Gilbert **Delahaye** ◆ M

martine

à la maison

casterman

Cet après-midi, les parents de Martine rendent visite à une amie.

– On fait un puzzle ? propose Jean.

– Bof. Les tiens sont trop faciles pour moi… et les miens, trop durs pour toi. Que dirais-tu d'une partie de Memory à la place ?

– Impossible, il manque des cartes…

Les deux enfants soupirent. Ils s'ennuient et ne savent pas quoi faire…

Tout à coup, Martine sourit.

– Je sais ! s'écrit-elle. On pourrait faire une surprise aux parents : nettoyer toute la maison pour leur retour !

– Bonne idée ! On commence par le salon ! Je recule les chaises pour faire de la place, et toi, tu passes l'aspirateur.

Le salon est tout propre ; maintenant, la cuisine !

Martine frotte le carrelage avec de l'eau et du savon.

– Patapouf, s'il te plaît, tu attends que le carrelage soit sec avant de descendre, pour ne pas tout salir !

La pièce la plus en fouillis... c'est la chambre de Martine!

Il y a des jouets partout!

Patapouf voudrait bien aider sa maîtresse, mais au premier jouet qu'il attrape... Boing! Le canard à ressort jaillit de sa boîte!

Pour nettoyer les habits, Martine a une idée.

– Viens voir, Jean, je vais laver les vêtements à la main, et toi, tu vas les essorer comme le faisait mamie, avec sa vieille essoreuse !

– Aïe ! C'est drôle de faire tourner ces rouleaux, mais c'est difficile ! souffle Jean en appuyant sur la manivelle. Il fallait être drôlement costaud, autrefois !

Une fois le linge étendu au soleil, Martine et Jean s'occupent de leur oiseau Topaze.

– Et si on posait sa cage sur le rebord de la fenêtre ? propose Jean.

– Bonne idée ! En plus, Moustache pourra lui tenir compagnie, répond Martine en souriant.

Ensuite, les enfants rentrent vite.

– Tu crois qu'on va devoir toutes les nettoyer ? demande Jean en regardant le tas de chaussures devant lui.

– Il ne faut brosser que celles en cuir. Oh... mais tu t'en es mis partout sur le visage ! Attention à ne pas salir tes vêtements, ça tache ! Regarde, même Patapouf est plus propre que toi... On dirait qu'il a trouvé chaussure à sa patte !

Plus que deux heures avant le retour des parents…

– Si on veut accueillir papa et maman avec un bon dîner, il faut d'abord faire la vaisselle.

– Allons-y ! Toi, tu laves, et moi, j'essuie, propose Jean.

– D'accord, mais frotte doucement. Si les assiettes te glissent des mains, notre petite surprise se transformera en grande bêtise !

Zut ! Il manque des ingrédients pour faire un bon dessert.

– Le voisin pourra sans doute nous dépanner, dit Martine.

Je lui téléphone.

– Voici du lait, du beurre et des œufs, annonce M. Dufrêne, qui sonne à la porte quelques minutes plus tard. La base de toute bonne pâtisserie !

Mais le lait ne sert pas qu'à cuisiner...

– Jimmy, Minette et Moustache ! appelle Martine.

C'est l'heure du goûter !

Les trois chatons accourent ! Et ils sont tous les trois très gourmands.

Et Patapouf, aime-t-il le lait ?

Au moment où les enfants ont tout nettoyé et commencent à cuisiner le repas du soir, voilà que la pluie se met à tomber.

– Une averse ! Vite, il faut rentrer le linge !

En moins de cinq minutes, le panier est rempli.

– Ah non, les chatons ! s'écrie Martine. N'en profitez pas pour faire les fous dans nos draps tout propres.

C'est bientôt l'heure du dîner.

– On pourrait faire des profiteroles, propose Jean, c'est le dessert préféré de maman.

– Bonne idée ! Suis la recette des choux dans le livre de cuisine. Pendant ce temps, moi, je m'occupe de la sauce au chocolat.

Bientôt, une odeur sucrée flotte dans la cuisine. Tout le monde s'en lèche les babines… surtout Patapouf !

Jean remplit les choux de crème, puis nappe la pyramide de bon chocolat chaud.

– Un vrai chef cuisinier, constate Martine. Tu mérites bien ta toque !

– Ouaf ! Ouaf ! intervient Patapouf, comme pour dire : « N'oubliez pas que je veux lécher la cuillère ! »

Il ne reste plus qu'à mettre la table.

Jean s'occupe des verres et Martine des serviettes.

– Je les plie en forme de fleur, dit-elle en s'appliquant, ce sera très joli.

– Papa et maman vont se croire au restaurant…

– Surtout si tu gardes ta toque ! réplique Martine avec un clin d'œil.

Cette fois, tout est prêt ! C'est l'heure des dernières vérifications !

– La maison est toute propre…

– … Le linge est propre, rangé et plié…

– … À nous aussi de nous faire beaux, histoire d'être aussi parfaits que notre maison !

– Oh non ! On a oublié quelque chose d'important ! Un beau bouquet à poser sur la table ! s'écrie tout à coup Martine, affolée.

– Ne t'inquiète pas, on n'a qu'à aller cueillir des roses et des œillets dans le jardin.

– Vite ! J'entends la voiture qui approche !

Les enfants n'ont même pas le temps de mettre les fleurs dans un vase...

– Bonsoir mes chéris ! lance maman en ouvrant sa portière.

– L'après-midi s'est bien passé ? demande papa.

– Oui, on a joué aux cartes… rien de plus… répond Martine avec un sourire malicieux.

• Découvre tous les titres disponibles dans ma mini-bibliothèque **martine** •

martine fait la cuisine
martine à la montagne
martine un amour de poney
martine petit rat de l'opéra
martine apprend à nager
martine au cirque
martine à la ferme
martine princesses et chevaliers
martine et les chatons
martine à l'hôpital
martine fête son anniversaire
martine et le prince mystérieux
martine à l'école
martine se déguise
martine et les quatre saisons
martine à la maison

Et retrouve toutes les aventures de **martine** dans la collection albums !

martine petit rat de l'opéra
martine garde son petit frère
martine baby-sitter
martine fête son anniversaire
martine l'arche des animaux
martine protège la nature
martine prépare une surprise
martine et les quatre saisons
martine et le prince mystérieux
martine est malade
martine à la maison
martine fête maman
casterman

Casterman
Cantersteen 47, boîte 4
1000 Bruxelles
Belgique

www.casterman.com

ISBN : 978-2-203-22441-4
N° d'édition : L.10EJCN000699.N001

D'après les albums de Gilbert Delahaye et Marcel Marlier.
Achevé d'imprimer en octobre 2020, en Roumanie, par Rotolito Romania SA, Sos.
(Cernica 47, 077145 Pantelimon Jud Ilfov, Bucarest, Roumanie)
Dépôt légal : janvier 2021 ; D.2021/0053/60
Déposé au ministère de la Justice, Paris (loi n°49.956
du 16 juillet 1949 sur les publications destinées à la jeunesse).

THE DE
TO

TWO INDIVIDUAL WALKS
OR
A 29 MILE CIRCULAR WALK OVER
THE TEN HIGHEST PEAKS /MOORLAND FELLS
WITHIN
THE PEAK DISTRICT NATIONAL PARK

AN
ESSENTIAL GUIDE TO
HELP YOU COMPLETE
THE
DERBYSHIRE TOP TEN

BRIAN SMAILES

You will never walk alone with these books published by Challenge Publications

Other books in this series

THE YORKSHIRE DALES TOP TEN
ISBN 0-9526900-5-5

THE LAKELAND TOP TEN
ISBN 0-9526900-3-9

Other books by the same author

THE SCOTTISH COAST TO COAST WALK
ISBN 0-9526900-8-X

THE COMPLETE ISLE OF WIGHT COASTAL FOOTPATH
ISBN 0-9526900-6-3

JOHN O'GROATS TO LANDS END
ISBN 0-9526900-4-7

THE NATIONAL 3 PEAKS WALK
ISBN 0-9526900-7-1

THE 1066 COUNTRY WALK
ISBN 1-903568-00-5

THE NOVICES GUIDE TO THE LYKE WAKE WALK
ISBN 0-9526900-1-2

THE YORKSHIRE 3 PEAKS WALK
ISBN 1-903568-01-3

MILLENNIUM CYCLE RIDES IN 1066 COUNTRY (EAST SUSSEX)
ISBN 1-903568-04-8

17 WALKS IN GLEN NEVIS
ISBN 1-903568-05-6

ISBN 1-903568-03-X

First Published 2001

CHALLENGE PUBLICATIONS
7, EARLSMERE DRIVE, BARNSLEY. S71 5HH
www.chall-pub.fsnet.co.uk
E mail challengepublications@yahoo.co.uk

The Author

Brian Smailes

Holds the record for the fastest 4 and 5 continuous crossings of the Lyke Wake Walk over the North York Moors. He completed the 210 miles over rough terrain on 5 crossings in June 1995 taking 85 hours and 50 minutes.

Brian lectures on outdoor pursuit courses and between these travels extensively on walking expeditions and projects around Great Britain.

Long distance running and canoeing are other sports he enjoys, completing 24 marathons and canoeing the Caledonian Canal 3 times.

ACKNOWLEDGEMENTS

In publishing this book I must thank the following people for their help and contribution :-

Pam Smailes for general support.

Geoff Whittaker & Janet Crossley for information/research.

Graham Fish for technical support.

Trevor Atkinson for accompanying me on this walk.

Eurotech Leisure Ltd, Walsall, West Midlands. For clothing and equipment supplied for the Derbyshire Top Ten.

ISBN 1-903568-03-X
First Published 2001

Published by:- Challenge Publications,
7 Earlsmere Drive, Barnsley, S71 5HH

Printed by:- Dearne Valley Printers Ltd. Tel: 01709 872188

CONTENTS

Useful Information

PHOTOGRAPHS

PLATE

Sketches

INTRODUCTION

The walks described in this book cover the ten highest peaks or moorland fells in Derbyshire. The routes take you on two circular walks over the Dark Peak area with impressive views from the hills and along the valleys. A large section of the route spans peat deposits and depending on the time of year and weather conditions, it can be very wet in places.

Three of the peaks have a 'trig' point on their summit while the others usually have a pile of stones marking the highest point. To the south of the A57 Snake Pass road there are seven of the top ten peaks with the other three on the northern side of the A57.

Along the suggested route you may find a number of other 'high spots' but as these are no more than 16m difference in height to the peaks shown and within 700m distance of the summit of the peaks, the author has not deemed their inclusion necessary.

The ten peaks can be walked either on a full day walk with an early start or on two separate walks consisting of seven and three peaks. The section between has been included separately.

All essential information to help you locate the peaks, timings, distances and grid references are all shown in detail with gradient profile, sketch maps and photographs to help you complete the top ten in a safe and enjoyable way.

The peaks in Derbyshire, although not as high as those in the Lake District, can be just as hazardous if you are not properly prepared and equipped for inclement weather. Follow the advice and recommendations in this book, complete the walk, then try the Yorkshire Dales and Lakeland Top Ten.

Recommended map

Ordnance Survey	Outdoor Leisure No.1
The Peak District	Dark Peak Area

Although this is the recommended map, you should ensure that whichever map you use it is relevant and up to date.

All compass bearings given in this book are shown as magnetic, 5° having been added to grid north.

ACCESS TO THE PEAK DISTRICT

By Road:- There are a number of main roads bordering the Peak District. The M1 takes you to the east of Sheffield, on reaching junction 31 turn onto the A57 which takes you to the Peak District.

To the south the Peak District is bordered by Matlock, Ashbourne and Leek and these can be quickly reached from Derby on the numerous access roads.

To the west of the Peak District is Manchester, and a convenient entry point to the area is from Glossop. Access from Manchester to Glossop is via the M60 circular motorway around Manchester heading east to the M67 following signs to Glossop on the A57.

To the north is Holmfirth and Huddersfield and a direct road from Huddersfield, the A616 takes you down to the outskirts of the National Park.

Once in the area there are car parks in and around Edale and parking areas on the A57 road. Many parking areas can be full especially at weekends and at peak holiday times.

By Rail:- There are stations at Sheffield, Glossop, Manchester, Chesterfield, **Edale, Bamford, Hathersage** and Stocksbridge. From here bus services operate to villages throughout the Peak District.

By Bus:- National coach companys operate services to the major towns and cities like Manchester, Sheffield, Chesterfield and Stockport. From these points you can take a local service to your intended destination.

There are a number of transport schemes to help reduce pollution, congestion and environmental damage to the National Park. The council and National Park Authority work closely together to encourage and promote the use of public transport in this area. When you plan your visit try to leave your car behind. Should you require bus times or fare information call 01332 292200.

THE PEAK DISTRICT NATIONAL PARK

This covers an area of 555 sq. miles at the southern end of the Pennines between Sheffield and Manchester. The park which was established in 1951 is one of the most heavily used and visited because it is easily accessible from the major conurbations of Sheffield, Manchester and Derby and in close proximity to major road networks. Approximately 38,000 people live in the park.

The Peak District Park is split principally into two areas, Dark Peak and White Peak. Although the walks featured in this book are in Dark Peak area, there are other areas throughout the National Park that are well worth exploring. Take time to explore the area and sample all that Derbyshire and the Dark Peak District in particular has to offer.

The ground beneath our feet consists mainly of millstone grit, laid down millions of years ago. This gritstone in some areas became exposed giving us the paths many people walk on today. These are known as edges, eg. Stanage Edge and The Edge.

Within the National Park it is estimated that there are approximately 5000 miles (8047km) of footpaths and bridleways. Some of these present a challenge to navigate, as they go over peat bogs and groughs. Modern day walkers have access throughout the National Park, but at the turn of the century most areas were private property. This has gradually changed over many years and people can now enjoy walking the hills and moorland in most areas of the park.

The National Park Authority employ many people not just in administration but as rangers who patrol the park and moors and negotiate and work with farmers with the aim of preserving the countryside for walkers, farmers, and all others who use the park for social and recreational purposes not forgetting those who live in the area.

Should you require more information on the National Park and Derbyshire generally, a list of contacts is given in the useful information section at the back of this book.

BRIEF HISTORY OF THE PEAK DISTRICT

The moors of the Peak District were originally covered with trees after the ice age, but these disappeared due to clearance and sheep grazing. The peat beds we see on the moors today were formed around 600BC from the remains of a type of moss called sphagnum moss which is now extinct.

Apart from the present day walkers and inhabitants of the Peak District, the area has a colourful history of ghosts and legends dating back to the Domesday book. There are stories of ghostly figures seen on the moors and of people who died in the great plague of 1665 appearing in the rectory at Eyam and other places.

Stories of large black dogs and more recently large black cats have regularly abounded in the villages surrounding the Peak District. The famous white lady who allegedly haunts the vicarage at Hathersage Church was seen one day by one of the clergy earlier this century, and in the same area Highlow Hall in Hathersage is reputed to be the most haunted house in Derbyshire.

Two of Derbyshire's most famous residents were Robin Hood, reputed to have been born in Loxley, Sheffield and Little John who resided in Hathersage and is buried in Hathersage churchyard. On Stanage Edge there is Robin Hoods cave, being famous as one of his hiding places.

On the top ten route, Kinder Downfall has its ghost of a one Jenny Crum who was drowned. The ghosts of her children may be seen visiting her at midnight on Easter eve. Strange noises and wailing can be heard on Kinder Scout and the clanking of armour on Bleaklow where Roman soldiers once passed by. These are only a few of the many ghost stories of this area.

The Peak District is also famous for numerous aircraft wrecks particularly from the 2nd world war, one of the more famous being a superfortress aircraft called 'over exposed' which was involved in nuclear testing during the war. It crashed on 3rd November 1948 on Higher Shelf Stones, just off the summit at G.R. 090950.

At James Thorn just off Higher Shelf Stones lie the wrecks of a Lancaster KB993 which crashed on 18th May 1945 at G.R. 077949 and a C47 Sky Train at G.R.082949 which crashed on 24th July 1945.

Aircraft wrecks litter the moors and just north of Bleaklow Hill is the wreck of a Defiant NB378 which crashed on 29th August 1941 at G.R. 103979. Just south of Crowden Tower is the wreck of a Anson NL185 which crashed on 23rd November 1945 at G.R. 089866.

All these wrecks add a new dimension to walking, or plane spotting while you complete the Top Ten although much of them have now disappeared due to the passage of time and the enthusiasm of souvenir hunters.

The village of Edale is perhaps more famous for the beginning or the end of the Pennine Way. Made famous by a certain Mr. A. Wainwright, this 250 mile high level route stretches to Kirk Yetholm in Scotland. It starts beside The Old Nags Head pub in Edale and runs along the backbone of England. Much of the route is wild and inhospitable but to walkers it presents a challenge that many people would one day like to take up.

The area of Kinder Scout may be remembered by walkers for a mass trespass which took place there on 24th April 1932 when walkers, angry at being denied access to large areas of the Peak District, deliberately descended in large numbers on the area. This action brought attention to the problem of access to the moors and generally increased public awareness of the problem.

There are many other tales to tell and things to see in the Peak District, but rather than try to tell it all now, I will leave it to you the walker to go to the area and find out for yourself.

PREPARATION

When preparing for this walk, you have to remember there is a proportion of climbing up and down, therefore knees and ankles should be in good working order before you leave.

Although the distance is only 29 miles, any walker attempting this walk needs to be reasonably fit, so training in the weeks before the walk is recommended. Start walking short distances two months before the event, gradually increasing the distance walked, ensuring you incorporate some hills into your training routes. Build up to 20 miles if possible during training, walking over rock, grass and moorland terrain. This training should ensure you are reasonably fit to complete the Derbyshire Top Ten.

Other types of fitness training e.g. cycling, keep fit sessions, jogging and swimming will all increase your fitness and stamina and help to prepare you for this walk.

Training in the use of basic map and compass work would be helpful, especially if the peaks and moors are covered in cloud as often happens in bad weather.

Consuming high energy food before and during the walk is most beneficial. Food with a high level of carbohydrate such as rice, pasta, potato, banana, malt loaf and milk will help to build up your energy reserves before the walk. While walking, glucose based sweets, apples and Kendal mint cake will all help to supply your body with extra energy, as will isotonic drinks.

Finally, from past experience, those who do some type of exercise and do not drink or smoke heavily, usually complete this walk. Those who do nothing and drive from A to B do not!

EQUIPMENT SELECTION

When considering equipment and clothing for this walk, you must remember that it may be a calm, still, and what seems like a nice day in Edale but nearing the summit of any hill it can be cold and very windy with low cloud. Often it is the wind chill factor that causes problems for walkers. With this in mind, the following suggested list of items should help you to both complete the walk and stay warm, dry and hopefully injury free.

1. Compass and guide book
2. Walking boots/fell boots
3. Walking socks including a spare set
4. Walking trousers (no jeans)
5. Warm upper body clothing (in layers), Spare clothing
6. Gloves, Woollen/fleece hat
7. Torch with spare bulb and batteries
8. Whistle, Note paper and pencil
9. Toilet paper
10. Survival bag
11. Basic first aid kit including plasters and vaseline
12. Fleece/waterproof fabric outer jacket/cagoul, overtrousers
13. Day rucksack
14. Food, Plastic drinks bottle (small)
15. Camera
16. Map of the area O.S. The Peak District, Dark Peak Area. No.1.

Use this as a checklist before you leave. In addition to the above items, a complete change of clothes should be available at the campsite/bed and breakfast or in your car ready for when you return.

Plate 1
The ascent of Grindslow Knoll.

Plate 2
The Mushroom Rock just off Grindslow Knoll.

THE BODY

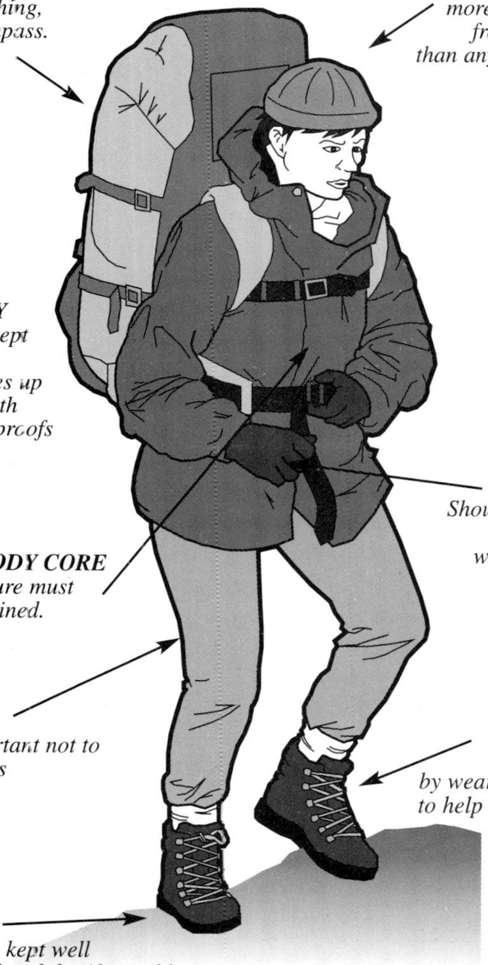
RUCKSACK
Containing food, drinks, first aid, clothing, map and compass.
THE HEAD
Should be kept warm, more heat is lost from the head than anywhere else.
THE BODY
Should be kept warm. Build clothes up in layers with wind/waterproofs on top.
HANDS
Should be kept warm with gloves.
MAIN BODY CORE
Temperature must be maintained.
LEGS
It is important not to wear jeans
ANKLES
Should be protected by wearing boots, to help strengthen them.
FEET
Should be kept well cushioned and dry if possible. Good fitting boots will help prevent blisters

HYPOTHERMIA

Hypothermia is caused when the body core temperature falls below 35°C. If a walker is not properly prepared for the conditions or the equipment/clothing is not satisfactory then a combination of the cold, wet, exhaustion and the wind chill factor can give a walker hypothermia.

Ways of Preventing Hypothermia

1 Build up body clothing in thin layers, adding on or taking off as necessary.
2. Have suitable wind/waterproofs with you.
3. Take some food/hot drink or boiled sweets which produce energy and heat during digestion.
4. Wear a balaclava/woolly hat to insulate the head, and some gloves.
5. Shelter out of the wind.
6. Take a survival bag and if conditions dictate, use it.

In any type of emergency/accident situation it is always advisable to come off high ground as soon as possible especially in fog, snow or other bad conditions. The temperature difference between the valley and the peak can be several degrees. If the injured walker is able to move safely, going down to lower ground is usually the best solution.

When conditions do not permit movement and if you are in a sheltered area, stay where you are until such time as conditions improve. It may be at this time that you put on extra clothing and use survival bags.

Plate 3
Crowden Tower and the path leading to it.

Plate 4
On route to Kinder Downfall.

Treatment for Hypothermia

1. Provide extra clothing and shelter from the elements.
2. Bodily warmth of others helps in a gradual warming.
3. If well enough come down into a warmer sheltered area.
4. Give hot drinks if conscious.
5. Give chocolate or sweets if the patient can still take food.
6. The casualty should be placed so that the head is slightly lower than the body.

DO NOT *rub the skin or use a hot water bottle as this can cause a surge of blood from the central body core to the surface, this could prove fatal.*

Alcohol should not be consumed on any walk and should not be given to anyone who has hypothermia. The body temperature will be lowered as well as giving a false sense of security.

WEATHER FORECASTS

It is important to check the weather forecasts before you leave. Doing this could save you from getting wet and cold or possibly doing the walk from start to finish in low cloud.

It is better to abandon the walk in snow/winter conditions than to risk lives out on the exposed peaks. The golden rule is be prepared and check the forecast before you go. Study the route carefully then decide if it is safe and sensible to complete the walk, or to wait and try another day, the peaks will still be there!

GRID REFERENCES

As a walker you will find it necessary at sometime to either find a place from a given grid reference or to make a grid reference from a place on a map.

All maps have grid lines running north/south and east/west. These are called 'Eastings' and 'Northings' and these lines have numbers on them. They can be further split into tenths, the numbers range from 00 to 99.

Grid references are normally given in six figures. The first three figures indicate how far to the east the place is. The second three figures indicate how far to the north the place is.

When making a grid reference look from left to right on a map and read the numbers going from left to right, write the numbers for the grid line to the left of your position, estimate the tenths to your position and write that number down to make 3 numbers.

Now look up your map and write the 2 numbers from the line just below your position. Repeat the second sequence as above. You should now have 6 numbers.

They are usually written as G R. 647556.

In using this method you should be able to pinpoint your target or position quite accurately on a 1:25000 scale map. Before you ascend the peaks you need to practise until you can both find grid reference points on a map and create a grid reference from a given position e.g. the grid reference for Mill Hill on the Pennine Way is 061904 using 6 figures and on map No.1 of the O.S. Outdoor Leisure Series, The Peak District.

Plate 5
Kinder Downfall. The path runs from right to left on the top.

Plate 6
Hern Stones

THE COUNTRY CODE

The countryside is a place where many people like to escape to and enjoy at various times. To do this we need to look after it when we use it and to preserve it for future generations.

The Peak District National Park is the most heavily used in the country so the following is a simple lists of do's and don'ts to help everyone enjoy the countryside.

Do

- Guard against all risk of fire
- Fasten all gates
- Keep dogs under close control
- Use gates and stiles to cross walls and fences
- Protect wildlife, trees and plants
- Take litter home
- Leave nothing but footprints, take nothing but photographs
- Be conscious at all times of erosion of footpaths

Don't

- Play radios etc. or create unnecessary noise
- Take mountain bikes on walkways
- Touch machinery, livestock or crops

THE DERBYSHIRE TOP TEN GRADIENT PROFILE

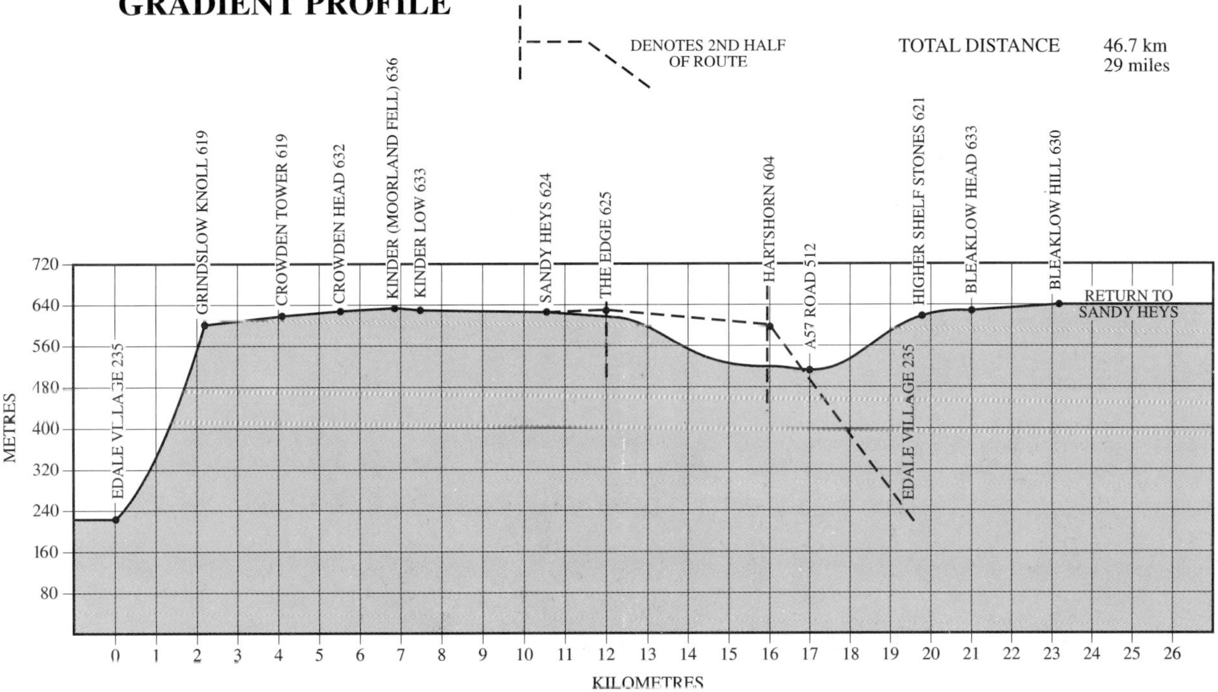

Plate 7
Bleaklow Head

Plate 8
A typical view of path which can be found throughout the Top Ten

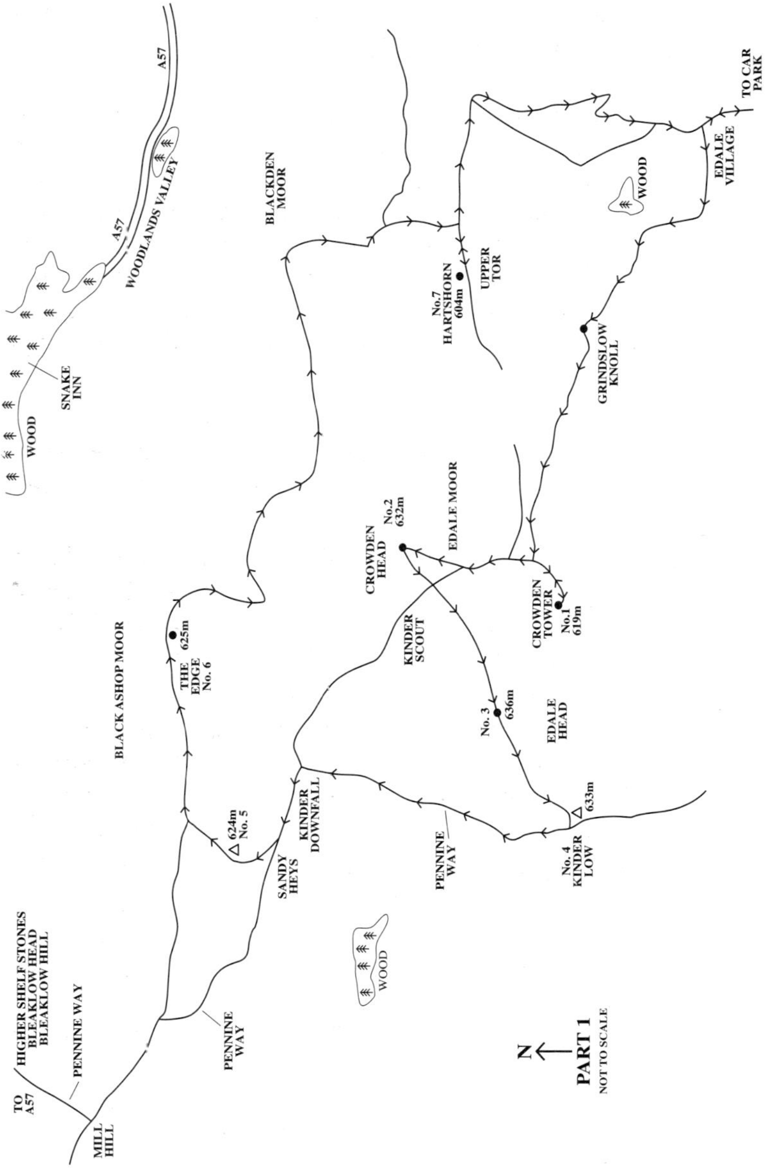
PART 1
NOT TO SCALE
N
TO CAR PARK
EDALE VILLAGE
WOOD
A57
WOODLANDS VALLEY
A57
BLACKDEN MOOR
No.7 HARTSHORN 604m
UPPER TOR
GRINDSLOW KNOLL
SNAKE INN
WOOD
EDALE MOOR
No.2 632m
CROWDEN HEAD
CROWDEN TOWER
No.1 619m
KINDER SCOUT
625m
THE EDGE No. 6
BLACK ASHOP MOOR
No. 3
636m
EDALE HEAD
633m
No. 4 KINDER LOW
PENNINE WAY
KINDER DOWNFALL
624m No. 5
SANDY HEYS
WOOD
HIGHER SHELF STONES BLEAKLOW HEAD BLEAKLOW HILL
PENNINE WAY
PENNINE WAY
TO A57
MILL HILL

PART 1
Crowden Tower, Crowden Head, Edale Head, Kinder Low, Sandy Heys, The Edge, Hartshorn

1. Leaving the car park in Edale, G.R.125853 turn right, walking under the bridge into Edale village. Pass the Rambler Inn (B&B). Field Head Campsite, visitor centre and rescue post are a little further on. You come to the Old Nags Head pub with hikers bar and the official start of the Pennine Way at the side of the pub.
2. As you approach The Old Nags Head pub, turn left following a sign towards Upper Booth and Pennine Way through a kissing gate.
3. Keeping the cottages to your left, continue ascending slightly going through a narrow opening in the fence, walking along the left side of a small stream, then through a small gate.
4. Follow a sign beside a stile to Grindslow Knoll, do not go over the stile. Your path runs by the side of several fields then ascends steeply across the hillside just above a small wood. You cross a stile as you start the main ascent, *(plate 1)*.
5. Just before the summit of Grindslow Knoll there is a pile of stones on each side of the path. A cairn or pile of stones marks the summit where there are excellent views to Crowden Tower and Kinder.
6. Leaving Grindslow Knoll, take bearing 296°M towards Crowden Tower which is 1.9km ahead. You come to a mushroom shaped stone at the side of the path just before a section of slabbed path over the moorland, *(plate 2)*. Your path then joins an alternative path from Grindslow Knoll a little further on. Just past this is a collection of large rocks resembling the face of a pig. Crowden Tower is a small rock face resembling a tower which you should see in front as you walk on the obvious path towards it, *(plate 3)*.

7. You cross a small stream then take the short ascent around the hillside to Crowden Tower. From the summit, retrace your steps back to the small stream you crossed just before the ascent to the Tower.

8. Walk towards Crowden Head, bearing 12°M from the stream where the path crosses it, following the course of the stream and in a direct line with Crowden Head. The path is undulating over the moor. Continue by the stream until you get to a point where a number of very large stones block the stream, then turn bearing 18°M from the large stones towards Crowden Head. Cross the undulating peat bogs which you may have to deviate round, looking ahead for a pile of stones which marks the highest point there, this is Crowden Head. You may see a post denoting a boundary line about 100m to your left as you walk to Crowden Head.

9. Take a bearing of 246°M from Crowden Head and walk in a direct line to Edale Head (636m) which is a pile of stones you should see on the highest point of land now ahead. Walk directly to it, again across the peat mounds and groughs.

10. Once you arrive at Edale Head (636m), you may see Kinder Low bearing 236°M and the 'trig' point there. Again continue on a feint path across the moor and peat in a straight line towards it. At Kinder Low there are numerous stones around resembling a moonscape, the number on the 'trig' point there is S4113. There are good views in all directions.

11. Follow a stony and uneven footpath, *(plate 4)* initially bearing 350°M from the 'trig' point, on the Pennine Way again, towards Kinder Downfall. This is a waterfall where the water usually blows back on itself which is rather unusual, *(plate 5)*. At Kinder Downfall there are a lot of large flat stones lying around and spectacular views down into the valley.

12. Keeping to the narrow path, walk around the top of Kinder Downfall anticlockwise for 800m, taking care, in the direction of Sandy Heys. Keep on the path then turn off walking a further 200m to the 'trig point No. 3443 near Sandy Heys.

At this point you can either continue the full route or complete the remaining two peaks in this section. The bridging section from Sandy Heys to Higher Shelf Stones can be found in part 3.

13. At Sandy Heys `trig' point take a bearing of 44°M to take you on a slight descent to the ridge south of Black Ashop Moor. On reaching the ridge, turn right walking for 1.1km to 'The Edge'. This narrow undulating path takes you along 'the edge' of the ridge which has good views into the valley to your left.
14. Take a bearing of 154°M from the highest point at The Edge to cut the corner, walking in a line across the moor to another ridge 400m further on. Turn right on meeting a narrow path along this ridge bearing 192°M on route to Hartshorn
15. Look for a path over a ford down to your left and up the other side at G.R.093892. As you near it, turn down to cross the ford and ascend to follow another ridge going clockwise for 3km before turning off the path at G.R.117882 which are the fords south of Blackden Moor.
16. Take a bearing due south to take you over the moor onto a slabbed path along the ridge of Upper Tor G.R.117877. On meeting this path, turn right walking 150m to the highest point at Hartshorn.
17. Returning to Edale, go back to the path above Upper Tor ridge and walk in an easterly direction to the turning leading down Golden Clough at G.R.125876.

Do not take this turning but branch off on bearing 202°M from that junction walking down and round the side of Ringing Rodger, this is at the side of the alternative route but is steep, and care should be taken.

18. Walk for 1.1km before taking a dog leg right down The Nab, then follow the man made path descending towards Edale. Cross a wooden stile then a field, to some steps leading to a footbridge over Grinds Brook.
19. You emerge onto a farm track which you follow for 150m back into Edale centre. Retrace your steps back through the village to the car park.

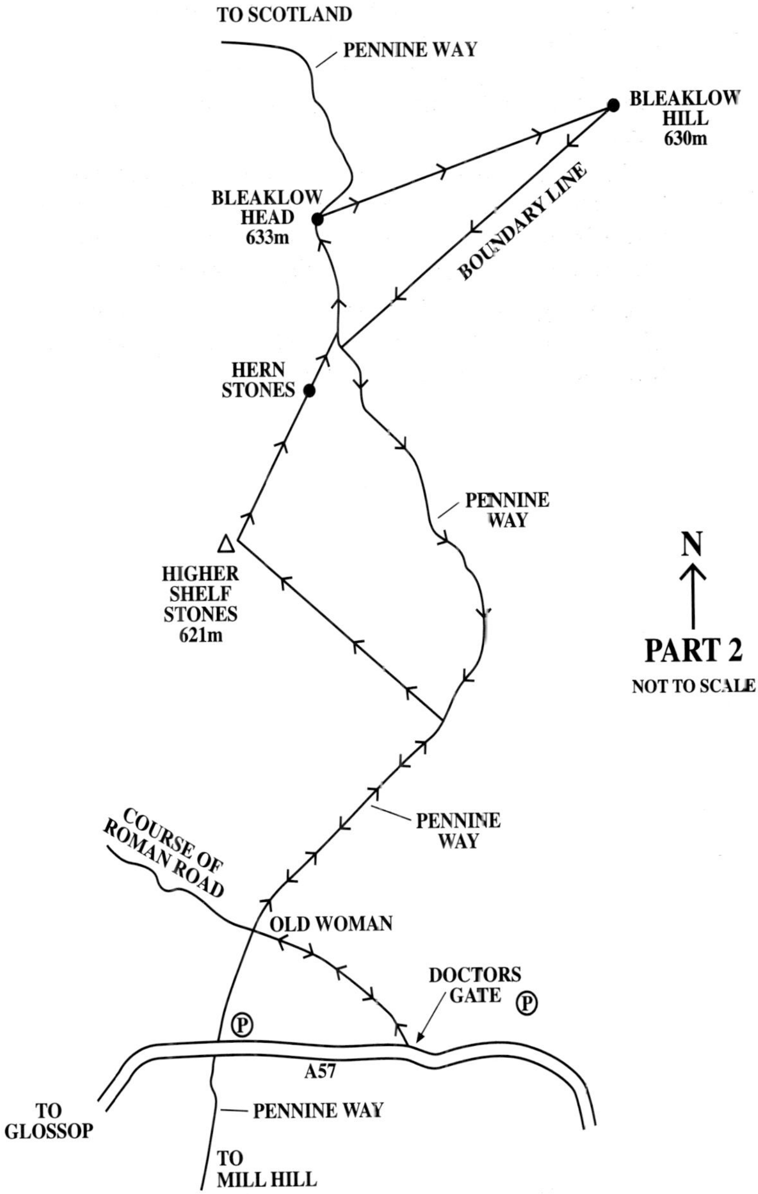
TO SCOTLAND
PENNINE WAY
BLEAKLOW HILL 630m
BLEAKLOW HEAD 633m
BOUNDARY LINE
HERN STONES
PENNINE WAY
N
HIGHER SHELF STONES 621m
PART 2
NOT TO SCALE
PENNINE WAY
COURSE OF ROMAN ROAD
OLD WOMAN
DOCTORS GATE
P
P
A57
PENNINE WAY
TO GLOSSOP
TO MILL HILL

PART 2
Higher Shelf Stones, Bleaklow Head, Bleaklow Hill

1. Park at Doctors Gate, (culvert), G.R.096929.
2. Go through the gate at the side of the small car park and follow the obvious narrow path, a former Roman Road, as it winds anticlockwise around the hillside in a N.W. direction for 800m to meet with the Pennine Way at a path crossing called Old Woman. You may see the A57 road 500m to your left.
3. Turn right on the Pennine Way bearing 45°M from the path crossing and walk for approx. 1.2km looking for a strip of grass path between the mounds of peat leading to Higher Shelf Stones on your left at G.R.089948.
4. Turn left from the Pennine Way at G.R.098942 and walk between the mounds and groughs, looking for the long strip of grass path ascending to the summit. A 'trig' point is on the summit built in among the rocks. Good views of Glossop in the valley and James Thorn, a rock outcrop in the same direction, can be had.
5. At the 'trig' point on Higher Shelf Stones take a bearing of 35°M to Hern Stones, *(plate 6)* an unusual rock formation on the moor. Walk over or around the numerous mounds of peat and groughs, keeping in the same general direction to Hern Stones, *(plate 6)*.
6. Keep the same bearing and walk until you rejoin the Pennine Way a short distance further on.
7. Turn left and continue on the Pennine Way ascending slightly to Bleaklow Head at G.R.092959, *(plate 7)*. Should the path disappear then keep heading for the higher ground a short distance ahead. The summit of Bleaklow Head is marked by a pile of loose stones on a large rock, *(plate 7)*. The Pennine Way should take you directly to Bleaklow Head.

8. When on Bleaklow Head, take a bearing of 74°M and walk for approx. 1.5km over or around the humps and mounds of peat. The groughs there can be wet and soft depending on recent rainfall. You arrive at Bleaklow Hill, G.R.105964, marked by a post on a mound of peat. This post is part of the boundary but is on the highest point.

9. On leaving Bleaklow Hill, take a bearing 237°M to take you along the boundary where you can follow the occasional post back to the Pennine Way. Look for the Hern Stones *(plate 6)* again in the same direction you are now walking.

10. On reaching the Pennine Way which is the obvious path you meet north to south just before Hern Stones *(plate 6),* turn left on a gradual descent again on the Pennine Way for 2.9km, walking along the course of a small stream and over several fords back to the Roman Road at G.R.090933 (Old Woman). At this point retrace your steps turning left back to Doctors Gate (culvert).

PART 3

Bridging Section, Sandy Heys to Higher Shelf Stones.

1. At the 'trig' point on Sandy Heys (624m) take a bearing of 252°M to take you back onto the Pennine Way. Once you are back on the path, follow the ridge round on a general bearing of 312°M for 1.3km to the end of the ridge, then descend for 860m to Mill Hill, G.R.061904. Much of the path from here to the A57 is slabbed.
2. Turn right bearing 36°M from Mill Hill walking for 3.4km following the Pennine Way over Moss Castle and Featherbed Moss to the A57 at Snake Pass. You may see traffic on the A57 road in the distance ahead as you approach from Moss Castle.
3. Cross the busy A57 road with care and continue on the Pennine Way for 1.6km before turning off to Higher Shelf Stones at G.R.098942, (see sketch map).

   Follow directions now from No. 4 in part 2 which will take you to Higher Shelf Stones, Bleaklow Head & Bleaklow Hill.

Bridging Section, Bleaklow Hill to The Edge.

1. On leaving Bleaklow Hill, take a bearing of 237°M to take you along the boundary where you can follow the occasional post back to the Pennine Way. Look for the Hern Stones again, *(plate 6)* in the same direction you are now walking.
2. On reaching the Pennine Way, which runs north to south, turn left on a gradual descent still on the Pennine Way walking for 3.1km back to the A57 road.
3. Cross the A57 with care, continue on the Pennine Way on the obvious path which is slabbed for most of the way. The path winds its way over the moor before a slight descent to Mill Hill.
4. Arriving at Mill Hill, turn left ascending the hillside for 860m to the top of the ridge. From this point take the left path, turning off The Pennine Way and walking along the edge of the ridge for 2.5km to The Edge.

Follow directions now from No. 14 in part 1 to take you to Hartshorn then Edale.

USEFUL INFORMATION

Grid Reference of Peaks/Moorland Fells

This section has been included to assist all walkers, particularly those who have a G.P.S. system to locate precise positions on route. You may find it helpful to use in connection with the relevant O.S. map of the area.

Crowden Tower	G.R.093870	*(plate 3)*
Crowden Head	G.R 096882	
Edale Head	G.R.086875	
Kinder Low	G.R 079871	
Sandy Heys	G.R.077894	
Higher Shelf Stones	G.R.089948	
Bleaklow Head	G.R.092959	*(plate 7)*
Bleaklow Hill	G.R.105964	
The Edge	G.R.092898	
Hartshorn	G.R.116877	
Grid Ref. of other principal points		
Grindslow Knoll	G.R.110868	
Kinder Downfall	G.R.084889	*(plate 5)*

Nearest Telephones

Snake Inn, Woodlands Valley	G.R. 112906
Kinder Road, Hayfield	G.R. 046868
Upper Booth	G.R. 103853
Yemans Bridge	G.R. 124853

Heights of Peaks

	mt.	**ft.**
Crowden Tower	619	2031
Crowden Head	632	2073
Edale Head	636	2087
Kinder Low	633	2077
Sandy Heys	624	2047
Higher Shelf Stones	621	2037
Bleaklow Head	633	2077
Bleaklow Hill	630	2067
The Edge	625	2050
Hartshorn	604	1982

Campsites in the Area

	Tel. No.
Mrs Cooper, Waterside Farm, Edale.	01433 670215
Cooper's Camp & Caravan Site, Edale.	01433 670372
Fieldhead Campsite, Edale.	01433 670386
Whitmore Lea Farm, Barber Booth.	01433 670238

A Selection of B&Bs

J Chapman, Brookfield, Edale, Hope Valley.	01433 670227
C Jackson, Mam Tor House, Edale, Hope Valley.	01433 670253
M Child, Rock Farm, Monks Road, Glossop.	01457 861086
Mill Farm, Edale Road, Hope, Hope Valley.	01433 621181
R Middleton, The White House, Shatton Lane, Bamford.	01433 651487
J Treacher, Pioneer House, Station Road, Bamford.	01433 650638

Youth Hostels

Edale	01433 670302
Crowden (Easter)	01457 852135
Castleton	01433 620235
Hathersage	01433 650493

Camping Barns

Edale, Cotefield Farm	01433 670273
Upper Booth, Upper Booth Farm	01433 670250
Glossop, Tanyard Farm	01457 857231
Castleton, Losehill Hall	01433 620373

Distances Between Prominent Landmarks
(Calculated to include ascents and descents)

	km	mls
Edale car park to Grindslow Knoll Summit	2.5km.	1.6
Grindslow Knoll Summit to Crowden Tower	1.9km.	1.2
Crowden Tower to Crowden Head	1.5km.	.9
Crowden Head to Edale Head	1.4km	1.2
Edale Head to Kinder Low	800m.	.5
Kinder Low to Kinder Downfall	1.9km.	1.2
Kinder Downfall to Sandy Heys	1km.	.6
Sandy Heys to A57 Snake Pass	5.7km.	3.5
A57 to Higher Shelf Stones	3.2km.	2.0
Higher Shelf Stones to Bleaklow Head	1.3km.	.8
Bleaklow Head to Bleaklow Hill	1.6km.	1.0
Bleaklow Hill to The Edge	12.9km.	7.9
The Edge to Hartshorn	3.9km.	2.4
Hartshorn to Edale car park	6.8km.	4.2
	46.4	29

Walking Times Between Prominent Points

Edale car park to Grindslow Knoll Summit	60 min
Grindslow Knoll Summit to Crowden Tower	35 min
Crowden Tower to Crowden Head	30 min
Crowden Head to Edale Head	32 min
Edale Head to Kinder Low	30 min
Kinder Low to Sandy Heys	75 min
Sandy Heys to Higher Shelf Stones	110 min
Higher Shelf Stones to Bleaklow Head	25 min
Bleaklow Head to Bleaklow Hill	25 min
Bleaklow Hill to The Edge	165 min
The Edge to Hartshorn	90 min
Hartshorn to Edale car park	50 min

The walking times shown above are approximate and will vary depending on fitness, weather conditions, weight of pack and number of walkers in group. They are shown only as a guide. To complete the ten peaks in 1 day will take approx. 11-14 hours walking time.

Tourist Information Centres

Ashbourne T.I.C. 13 Market Place, Ashbourne.	01335 343666
Bakewell T.I.C. Bridge St. Bakewell.	01629 813227
Buxton T.I.C. The Crescent, Buxton.	01298 25106
Castleton Information Centre Castle Street, Castleton.	01433 620679
Chesterfield T.I.C. Low Pavement, Chesterfield.	01246 345777/8
Edale Information Centre Edale Centre.	01433 670207
Fairholmes Information Centre (Derwent Valley)	01433 650953
Glossop T.I.C. Victoria St. Glossop.	01457855920
Leek T.I.C. Market Place, Leek.	01538 483741
Macclesfield T.I.C. Town Hall, Macclesfield.	01625 504114
Matlock Bath T.I.C. The Pavilion, Matlock Bath.	01629 55082
Matlock T.I.C. Crown Square, Matlock.	01629 583388
Torside Visitor Centre. Longdendale Valley.	(No Tel No.)

Useful Addresses/Telephone Numbers

Long Distance Walkers Association
Brian Smith
10 Temple Park Close, Leeds LS15 0JJ
Tel: 0113 2642205
This association is set up to further the interests of those who enjoy long distance walking. Members receive a journal three times each year which includes information on all aspects of long distance walking.

Ramblers Association
2nd Floor, Camelford House,
87-90, Albert Embankment, London SE1 7TW
Local groups with regular meetings.

Walks With A Ranger Hotline 01629 815185

Derbyshire Bus Line 01298 23098 or 01332 292200

Rail Information 0345 484950

Challenge Publications Web Site :-
chall-pub.fsnet.co.uk
Email:- challengepublications@yahoo.co.uk

Car Parking

Edale	G.R.125853
Door Clough	G.R.107848
Bowden Bridge	G.R.048869
A57 Snake Pass	G.R.088929
Doctors Gate (culvert)	G.R.096929

Public Houses/Inns

The Snake Inn, A57	G.R.112906
The Rambler Inn, Edale Village	G.R.123855
The Old Nags Head Pub, Edale Village	G.R.123860

Glossary of Words

B&B - Bed and breakfast.

Bearing - A degree or number of degrees set on a compass then follow the direction of travel arrow to walk on that bearing to reach your intended destination.

Cairn - An ancient stone mound erected as a marker. Often modern day piles of stones are referred to as cairns. This is not the case but many people use this expression when referring to piles of stones that denote a path or route.

Crag - A steep rugged rock or peak.

Dyke, Dike, Ditch - Words used to denote a long ridge of earth or a water channel either raised up or below normal level.

G.P.S. - Global Positioning System, used more frequently by walkers to locate precise positions. Extremely useful in low visibility.

Grid Reference - Derived from the National grid reference system. This is used to pinpoint a place on a map by the use of letters and numbers, written as G.R. _ _ _ _ _ _

Groughs - A channel cut into the soft surface usually by running water.

Kissing Gate - Swing gate that usually lets one person through at a time by moving the gate backwards and forwards.

Magnetic Bearing - This is a grid bearing taken from a map and the relevant magnetic variation added to it to obtain the magnetic bearing. See the relevant maps for details of current magnetic variation.

Metalled Road - Generally known as a stone chipping road. This term evolved and became known as the roads metal or the roads surface.

Outcrop - Part of a rock formation that sticks out from the main body of rock.

Path - A narrow path of grass, mud, stone etc. suitable for walkers. Not usually more than 2m wide.

Summit - The highest point of a mountain or hill.

T.I.C. - Tourist information centre.

Track - A road (possibly rough) usually wide enough for a vehicle and often leading to a farm.

'Trig' Point - True name is triangulation pillar. These mark the summit of many mountains, but not every mountain has one. It is a small stone pillar with a number on it. The height of the mountain is taken from this point.